With Love from My Dad - A Collection of Humorous Verse

- MARGARET RATTRAY -

An environmentally friendly book printed and bound in England by
www.printondemand-worldwide.com

FSC Mixed Sources
Product group from well-managed forests, and other controlled sources
www.fsc.org Cert no. TT-COC-002641
© 1996 Forest Stewardship Council

PEFC Certified
This product is from sustainably managed forests and controlled sources
PEFC/16-33-415
www.pefc.org

This book is made entirely of chain-of-custody materials

FastPrint Publishing
www.fast-print.net/store.php

With Love from My Dad - A Collection of Humorous Verse

ISBN 978-178035-380-7

First published 2012 by
FASTPRINT PUBLISHING
Peterborough, England.

Contents

Contents

I would like to thank my family and friends for the help and encouragement they have given me regarding the publishing of my books.

Bill and Muriel Dawson for proof reading and Joyce Wells for formatting to ready to print.

The main person I have to thank of course is my dad as without his input there would be no book, so thanks dad.
He was always a fantastic dad and it is great that I can still hear from him on such a regular basis.

Artwork by Margaret Rattray

A Dram Or Two

I do not know the way to go.
The road to me, you have to show
I cannae even mind my name
Isn't that an awful shame.

The night wis just like any other,
I reached the pub, it was no bother.
In the door, climb on ma stool,
Why start now to break the rule.

Some amber liquor in ma gless,
With everyone, I remember less.
I did not think of my head next day,
The drink affects ye in that way.

A few more glesses, soon ye'll find,
Lots o' things ye cannae mind.
Everyone becomes your friend,
A really must be roond the bend.

They're happy all to take ma drink,
It's getting really hard to think.
My mind is going round and round,
So are the walls and so's the ground.

Reach in ma pocket, money's done.
I cannae afford another one.
So aff ma stool and oot the door,
But tomorrow night, I'll be back for more.

A Trip Tae The Park

When I was young, I went tae the park
I thought it would be quite a lark
So first I climbed upon the chute
I slid doon fast and cam shootin oot.

I landed smack upon my rear
The pain it gave, I didnae fear,
But the hole in ma breeks that I tore
I knew would hurt me even more.

I knew I would have tae face ma maw
When the hole in ma breeks she finally saw
I couldnae think o' any excuse
That she hadnae already heard me use.

Already in trouble, I had nothing to lose
So I knew I could try, whatever I choose.
So I jumped on a swing, soared up high
I felt that I could really fly.

But I flew right off and fell in a pool
It was muddy water and I felt a fool,
A found that I was drippin wet.
So there's no point in going home yet.

The roundabout was going fast
But I managed tae jump on it at last
But it was going round sae quick
I suddenly started tae feel sick.

A Trip Tae The Park

This roundabout I'll hae tae stop
I'll stick oot a leg and let it drop
I know the very thing to do
I'll stop it wi the tae o' ma shoe.

It stopped the roundabout no doubt
But I very quickly also found out
There was nae tae left in ma shoe
I knew there would be a hullabaloo.

So I dawdled hame very slow,
As I knew no mercy maw would show,
She gave one look and then a shout
You silly, stupid, little lout.

You know tae me ye are a disgrace
I dinnae want tae see yer face
So tak yersel up tae yer bed
And again tonight ye won't be fed.

A Trip Tae The Pictures

I went to the pictures
And this is what I saw,
Loads and loads o' people,
Champin wi their jaws.

Muckle bags o' sweeties,
Clutched in every hand,
A wisnae feelin jealous,
Ye have to understand.

O' their bulgin bags o' popcorn,
Or their cans o' fizzy water,
Both ma hands were empty,
But that really didnae matter.

Until the usherette cam roond
Wi a her lovely wares
Ma girl cam back, wi a lovely cone,
A said come on fair shares.

A lick to you and a lick to me.
Seemed such a clever thought.
But ma luck wis really oot that night
And a lesson I was taught.

If ye want a lick, go buy yer ain,
Ye'r getting nane o' mine.
A got the message right enough
She laid it on the line.

A Trip Tae The Pictures

She licked and licked, wi flappin tongue,
Till nothing there wis left.
I simply sat beside her,
Feeling quite bereft.

But what she didnae realise
Ma money wisnae done
And on the homeward journey,
It'll be fish and chips for one.

A Tiny Fly

A tiny fly flew in ma e',
Suddenly I couldnae see.
I blinked away to no avail
I'll try to get it by the tail.

But there wis no tail upon this fly,
The one that just flew in ma eye,
So I'll just have to let it be,
The fly that flew intae ma e'.

A Wee White Moose

One day ma pal gave me a moose.
I sneaked it in the hoose.
I had it in a cardboard box.
It widnae need nae locks.

A moose ye see, is awful wee,
It widnae manage to get free.
I hid it carefully in ma chest,
The less ma mither knew the best.

She had a thing ye see for mice.
Her words indeed were quite precise.
Filthy vermin, they carry germs,
Were just a couple o' her terms.

But that wee moose wis very bright,
A soon found oot that very night.
It ate its way, right through ma box,
It nibbled an chewed ma pants and socks.

It climbed right up and oot the drawer,
It must have wanted to explore.
It ran across ma bedroom floor
And very quickly oot the door.

It must have gone right doon the stairs
But I wis sleepin unawares.
The first I knew, I heard a scream
It wis too real to be a dream.

A Wee White Moose

I ran doon and through the hall,
No feelin very brave at all.
My maw wis standin on a chair
Starin at the kitchen flair.

A saw a moose, a filthy beast
In ma pantry havin a feast.
It wis pure white, it wisnae wild
A'm sure a have to blame you child.

Just tell to me where it came from
Did you bring it intae ma home
Noo dinnae tell me any lees,
That thing will be fu o' disease.

All hae to throw oot a ma food,
A know it will nae be nae good.
A have nae money for any mair.
But you can starve for all I care.

I cannae believe ye'd be sae silly,
We named ye well when we cried ye Billy.
You'll regret the day ye got that moose,
And brought it home into ma hoose.

Bath Night

I wis sittin in the bath one night
Feelin kind o bored,
I saw a bottle by the tap
Which into the bath I poured.

I wisnae sure o the amount tae use
So I just poured in the lot,
But the bubbles quickly started to rise
An an awful fright I got.

They poured right ower the side o the bath
And ran across the floor.
And as the bubbles spread some more,
They quickly ran beneath the door.

I loudly shouted tae ma maw
Come up a need some help.
A knew a had a bare behind
An I knew I'd get a skelp.

A heard her footsteps on the stair,
Then the door was opened wide
An as her feet cam in the door
I saw her start tae slide.

She clattered doon wi an awful thump
As she landed on the flair
She let oot the maist awful yell
And I know that fall wis sair.

Bath Night

And as she tried tae scramble up
She went head first in the watter
And as she fell the watter rose
Where it went it didnae matter.

A scrambled oot as fast as I could
Water spreading far and wide
I knew there wis only one thing to do
Try tae find a place tae hide.

Don't you think you can leave this hoose
A've done the washin for tomorrow
Unless ye go oot in yer birthday suit
You'll have tae find some clothes tae borrow.

So the moral of this sorry tale
Strange bottles do not try.
Or you may early, land in bed
And on your pillow, tears you'll cry.

Building Ma Den

Ma face wis black, ma hands were sair
But I dug away without a care
A thought a'd make a den ye see,
Big enough just for me.

A dug away deep in the soil,
A found it wis a real hard toil,
A gave a stretch, oh mercy me
This is harder than a thought it would be.

A bent ma back and dug some mair,
Noo everything wis getting sair,
But the hole it wis getting deep,
A didnae think it wis sae steep.

But when I tried to climb right oot,
I slipped and fell back tae the foot,
The more a tried, the worse it got,
The earth wis cavin in a lot.

It all fell in and buried me,
Just ma luck, it's time for tea,
But just when a thought ma luck was out,
I heard ma faither gie a shout.

Where have ye gone, ye silly lad,
Just you answer, its yer dad,
So a gave a shout and he rescued me
And a got hame in time for tea.

Cats, Cats, Cats

Tabby cats, stripey cats
Some as black as soot,
White cats, grey cats
And some that don't get oot.

Fat cats, thin cats
Some wi mangy hair,
Others are aristocrats
With noses in the air.

Manx cats, stray cats
Some are Siamese,
Persian cats and tam cats
All designed to please.

Good cats, happy cats
Some wi gentle paws,
Wild cats, angry cats
Cats wi scratchy claws.

I never was a lover
Of any kind of cat
I got myself a dog instead
And lavished love on that.

Cats, Nothing But Cats

There's cats, cats nothing but cats
They lie on the chairs, the beds and the flair,
There's a lovely garden just oot the back
If it wis up tae me I'd put them oot there.

But not oor Elizabeth who pampers and pets
Treating them all like they stayed at the Ritz.
Crunchies for this one, fish for another,
If it wis up tae me, they'd be scrapin for bits.

Look at them scratchin, is it the fleas,
Out wi the combs to draw through their hair.
The back and front, then its the legs,
If it wis up tae me I'd shave them all bare.

They clatter oot doors and rattle back in,
They scratch the chairs, scrape at the floors,
One even leaves dirty feet in the sink,
If it wis up tae me I'd show them the door.

But they're lucky cats, you must agree,
Plenty of love and running free.
I hope they know how lucky they are,
As they could have been owned by me.

Caught In The Rain

I wis caught in the rain ae day
It cam on unexpected,
I hadnae on a hat or coat
So I wisnae well protected.
The rain it battered doon sae hard
I soon wis soaked right through.
It ran in rivers doon ma back
And tae places oot o view.
My shoes they soon were soakin wet
They squelched with every stride
I broke in to a faster run
I'll need to get inside.
It didnae matter how fast I ran
The rain fell faster still.
If I don't get hame and oot o these clothes
I'll end up with a chill,
The rain it drippit oot ma hair
It drippit oot ma clothes
And just to help to make things worse
Water drippit oot ma nose.
At last I got inside ma hoose
And strippit aff ma clothes
I saw that I was turning blue
From my head down to my toes.
I had a bath and went to bed
But still I caught the flu,
So always take a hat and coat
Then this won't happen to you.

Fun In The Snow

The snow wis fallin really fast
I'll hae some fun wi it at last.
I ran off quickly doon the street
Hopin for some pals to meet.

The snow ye see is no much fun
If ye find yersel the only one.
You need to find a pal or two
To join in all the fun with you.

We made some snowballs first of all,
Some were big and some were small
But I threw one at wee Jackie's jaw
And he ran off hame to tell his maw.

We then went sledgin on the hill
That really was an awful thrill.
But wee Tam fell off and hit his head
And had to go hame to his bed.

A snowman then we tried to make
But that really wis a big mistake
We took wee Geordie's hat and scarf
And he didnae think that was a laugh.

Now there's only me and Jim and Joe
We soon decided where to go.
We'll make a slide along the street,
Watch folk slippin aff their feet.

Fun In The Snow

Up and doon we slid and slipped
Our excitement never dipped
And as the time began to pass
Our slide became like polished glass.

Along the street came postman Jack
And soon he was lyin on his back
His letters landed in the snaw,
He wisnae very pleased at a.

But there was someone heard his shout
And quickly rushed to help him out
Just our luck it was Sergeant James
And he quickly shouted out our names.

Ye'd better run, I'll be roond soon,
I'll be at yer doors this afternoon,
When yer faither hears what a have to say,
Ye'll rue the fun ye had today.

I Went Tae The Gym

I looked in the mirror, the other night
An saw ma big fat tum.
Maybe I should join a gym
And have a go at losing some.

So off I went tae the gym next day
Said a wanted tae enrol
I quietly smiled tae myself
This should be just a stroll.

They took me to another room
Trainers stood there in a line,
A hulkin brute o' six foot ten
Said a'll tak him, he'll dae just fine.

We'll start with something easy,
Just running on the spot,
That will maybe tell me
What stamina you've got .

I started off at quite a pace
This really is quite hard
The trainer then yelled out at me
Ye'r like a great big lump o lard.

Now here's a box, jump on and off
I'll count how much you can
But after three a drappit doon
An he cried what a specimen o' a man.

I Went Tae The Gym

Then he handed me a metal bar
This isnae lookin great,
Then at either end, he stuck some weights
Now a really think I've met ma fate.

I lifted the weight as much as a could
But it belted off ma nose
So as fast as I could I dropped it
An it nearly landed on ma toes.

By now I'd really had enough
Ma body a wis sair
So a decided tae stay just as a wis
I really didnae care.

So off I went, to the shop next door
And said with a great big sigh
I'd like to place an order
For some double chips and pie.

It's A Poem Fae Yer Daddy

It's a poem fae yer daddy
He's a master at this art,
As once again his genius,
To you he will impart.

I really was a handsome lad
Wullie was ma name,
But it was ma skill at poetry,
That gave to me ma fame.

I wrote some on a desk at school,
The words they were so grand,
But the teacher didnae think the same
And she took me by the hand.

She took me to the heidie,
A bruiser o' a man.
He took his belt oot o' a drawer.
I quickly turned and ran.

My luck was really oot that day,
I stumbled, then I fell,
He drew his belt doon on ma hand,
You should have heard me yell.

It swelled up to the size of two,
Twas red as any fire.
The boys all queued up round about,
So my hand they could admire.

It's A Poem Fae Yer Daddy

When I then got home from school,
My mum asked what I'd done,
But I didn't expect the words she said,
I'm ashamed of you my son.

Aff to bed you now can go,
Nae supper will ye get
And when yer dad gets hame fae work,
He'll no be pleased I bet.

Sure enough on the stroke of seven,
My dad come through the door,
He gave me such an awful swipe,
He knocked me on the floor.

When ma brothers heard ma tale,
They laughed out loud in glee,
The only thing they had to say,
Wis a'm glad it wisnae me.

Now that's the end of ma sorry tale,
My single claim to fame
And if you do not want my fate.
Don't ever sign your name.

It's All The Rage

I came across a book one day
It was full of information
I'll follow it down to a T,
Just think of the transformation.
It told you how to dress in style
Even showed you clothes to wear.
There were even lots of pages
Of styling for your hair.
I took the scissors to my hair,
I followed every page
The caption at the start it said
This is all the rage.
To my wardrobe, next I went
To do some alterations
I cut and sewed and snipped away
It was a new creation.
When at last the job was done
I looked at it in pride
I cannot keep this to myself
I'll take a trip outside.
But once outside, folk stood and stared
Then everybody laughed
What on earth is that you've on
Don't you know you look right daft.
My book had said, it was all the rage
I'll need to check once more.
But when I looked at the opening page
The date was nineteen forty four.

Its All Untrue

One day when I was late for school
I thought I'd tell a lee
Ma maw is ill, and in her bed
So she wisnae able tae waken me.

Oh dear what's wrong, the teacher said
I can maybe call round later.
Do you have any food in yer hoose
And someone who can cater.

I can get the cook tae bake some pies
And to maybe make a stew,
Some home made bread and treacle scones
Then maybe add a cake or two.

I then got feart and started to cry
And he said, now don't be sad
So I knew I had to tell him
As my maw she would be mad.

So I stammered as I told him
That I had told a lee
You nasty little beggar
Did ye think that ye could lee tae me.

I've met your type afore you see,
I've heard it many times.
So when you get hame fae school the night
You can write five hundred lines.

Mother's Revenge

It was a bright and sunny day,
A thought that I'd go oot tae play,
I went for a wander doon the street,
Hoping my two pals I'd meet.

There's Tam and Geordie wi their ba'
Kickin it against a wa'
I quickly joined them in their game,
Thinkin this is awful tame.

Suddenly I took a run,
I'll make this game a bit more fun,
Using all the skills I knew,
I kicked the ball and off it flew.

Ower the wall and out of sight,
Geordie said that wis just spite,
Ye better go and find ma ba'
Before I punch ye on the jaw.

I quickly clambered ower that wa'
But I couldnae see the ba' at a'
Then I looked up in a tree.
There was the ball in front of me.

I shook the tree, poked up a stick,
I even threw a muckle brick,
But I wis simply out of luck.
The ba' was well and truly stuck.

Mother's Revenge

The only way to get it free,
Wis to climb into the tree.
I climbed the tree, just like a chimp,
I'll show to them I am no wimp.

But then a branch, it tore ma breeks,
An I wis showin ma bare cheeks,
I found that I wis stuck right fast.
I knew ma luck just couldnae last.

I shouted oot tae Geordie and Tam.
Get some help as quick as ye can,
Go doon the road and get ma dad,
Even though he will be mad.

Up came ma dad, he brought his ladder
I'd never seen him any madder.
What a stupid thing to do,
Why does it always happen to you.

He put his ladder against the tree,
At last I thought, I'll soon be free,
But that ladder didnae stretch,
I still wis two foot out o' reach.

I'll need to phone the fire brigade,
And they may come, to your aid,
Yer mum and me wont live this doon,
The story will soon be roond the toon.

Mother's Revenge

The firemen brought me to the ground,
I stood there shakin, not a sound.
What dae ye say tae these kind men,
For getting you back doon again

I said do you think ye could get ma ba'
Or I winnae hae nae friends at a',
Hae nae friends, ye wee tyke,
Dad said to me as he gave a swipe.

Where's the manners ye were taught,
Noo mair shame to us ye've brought,
After a' yer silly pranks,
I thought at least ye wid say thanks.

I said ma thanks and home we went,
There to my room, I wis sent.
Tak aff yer breeks, look at that tear,
I'll have to do a quick repair.

Ma mum looked through her mending box,
Materials and bits o' socks,
At last she found a blue to match
And quickly she sewed on a patch.

But there were flowers on that square,
She said to me I dinnae care,
That to me is no concern,
Its time that you began to learn.

Mother's Revenge

So now I have to go to school,
Lookin like a silly fool.
I'm the only one who has a patch,
That wi their trousers disnae match.

The Chippie

A went tae the chippie for ma tea
Chips an crispy fish in batter
The man he asked, dae ye want some sauce
But a said, it didnae matter.

Just loads o' salt and vinegar
Poured on ma fish an chips,
The very thought o' that lovely feast
Made me lick ma lips.

That parcel it wis piping hot
In paper it wis wrapped.
A'll just go roond an visit ma pal
And on his door a chapped.

But he had a great big hairy dug
And it bounded ower tae me
He grabbed the parcel fae ma hands
And he had ma fish and chips for tea.

My Bike

When I was young I had a bike,
Like any other it was quite unlike,
I built it all by myself you see,
All the bits I found for free.

I found the frame inside a skip,
When I wis prowlin round the tip.
It had nae brakes, it had nae seat,
Nae wheels or pedals for ma feet.

I took it hame that very day,
Then went doon the den tae play,
There I saw to my surprise,
A sight that gladdened up ma eyes.

Someone else had left a cart,
It wisnae looking very smart.
But it had a pair of wheels,
That very nearly looked ideal.

I added them onto ma frame,
They almost looked the same,
Then I chanced upon a seat,
Beside a bucket doon the street.

Now all I need are pedals two
And a handlebar that is'nae new.
A neighbour doon the road fae me,
Said I can gie ye them for free.

My Bike

The frame wis red, the pedals green,
The seat the brightest blue I've seen,
One wheel wis yellow, one tyre wis flat,
You've never seen a bike like that.

I got a pump, to fix the tyre,
Blew it up, higher and higher,
Then I jumped upon the seat
And pedalled off along the street.

I very soon got in ma stride,
Excitement gripped me deep inside.
The wheels were going round and round,
Making a lovely whishing sound.

I very soon came to a hill,
Free wheeled down, what a thrill,
But when I went to use the brake,
I soon discovered ma mistake.

There were no brakes upon ma bike
And soon I ran into a dyke.
I went flying through the air,
About the pain I didnae care.

Ma bike ye see withstood the crash,
It only had a wee bit bash,
So we both lived to tell the story,
Of that bike and all its glory.

My Birthday

Last week it was ma birthday
And I asked my friends for tea.
When every one of them arrived
They had a present just for me.

I ripped them open one by one
To see what was inside.
There were lots of lovely gifts
And my smiles I could not hide.

Brand new pyjamas, slippers too
Then a car with shiny wheels
A cuddly toy to take to bed
How soft that teddy feels.

Lots of books and pencils too,
This really is great fun
So I just kept on ripping
Until they all were done.

We played some games
Made lots of noise
When I let my friends
Play with my toys.

Very soon it was time for tea
We all rushed to the table,
Just tuck in, enjoy yourselves
And eat what you are able.

My Birthday

There were sausages and little rolls
Crisps and cakes and biscuits too,
Jelly, trifle, chocolate sponge
Soon disappeared from view.

But I really was a greedy lad
Eating too much cake and jelly
So I landed early in my bed
As my eyes were bigger than my belly.

My Jam Tart

I thought one day I would be smart
An steal a bit o' maw's jam tart.
She soon found out that some had gone
And said to me, now tell me son.

Wis it you that a piece of my tart did take
Tell the truth for your own sake,
So I looked at her, straight in the eye
An told her a great big dirty lie.

It wisnae me that ate the tart
But that really wisnae very smart
As I really could not fool ma maw
As the jam wis stickin tae ma jaw.

My Brand New Tammy

I got a brand new tammy,
I stuck it on ma head,
I wouldnae take it off again,
I wore it to my bed.

I got it fae ma granny,
She knitted it for me.
I went there on a Sunday,
And I always stayed for tea.

I had fish fingers, chips and peas
And lots of lovely cake,
She was a lovely cook ma gran
And all the cakes she'd bake.

I always had a lot of fun
Each time I went to stay,
She always took me to the park,
Where I could run and play.

I really love my granny
And my granny she loves me
And that's why every Sunday,
I go round there for my tea.

My Dancing Lessons

I thought that I should learn to dance
To leap and turn and lively prance.
I could then the girls impress
As I showed off, my finesse.
The ballet first is what I'll try,
Through the air I'll leap and fly.
But then the silly tights I wore,
Decided me to try no more.
So then I thought the highland fling,
But I didnae hae nae swords to bring.
I jumped ower lines drawn on the floor,
It seemed to me an awful bore.
The jive it had me in a twist,
The teacher held me by the wrist,
A lively turn, fly through the air,
The landing wis sae awful sair.
Then I thought I'd try the tango,
Might as well be the fandango.
The waltz and samba fared nae better
Though I stuck it to the letter.
Then I met a girl called Lizzie,
Who spun me round till a wis dizzy,
She quickly taught me every move
Till her and I cut quite a groove.
Now no more lessons do I need,
Life for me has changed indeed.
I don't have time, I am too busy.
Every night I'm courting Lizzie.

My Special Date

One day I had a special date
Wi a lassie in ma class,
I eyed her surreptitiously
When ever I would pass,

I never thought for a minute
That she would look my way,
But I struggled very manfully
For some words to her to say.

Many times I strode up close
But as I just got near,
The words they all dried in my mouth
And I crumpled up in fear.

But at last I found the courage
To ask Jeannie on a date,
I said to her seven thirty
And please do not be late.

Now it's the day and nearly time
Dressed up in Sunday best,
Hair all combed and tidy,
Now comes the crucial test.

A last glance in the mirror
That's when I really froze
For shining like a beacon
Wis a great plook on ma nose.

My Wee Hen

When I wis wee, I had a hen.
I kept her in a wire net pen.
She laid an egg each day for me,
I had it fried or boiled for tea.

Then came a day I had to beg,
For ma hen it hadnae laid ma egg.
Please lay ma egg I will be good
For yer eggs they are ma favourite food.

I gave her water, checked she wis fed,
Put fresh straw into her bed.
I asked ma hen if she wis sad,
Perhaps I had done something bad.

She looked at me with beady eyes
Then turned her back to my surprise.
Maybe I know what's wrong with you,
Perhaps you need a friend or two.

So I built ma hen a bigger pen,
And got three chickens for ma hen.
Now she's happy as can be,
And I get ma egg again for tea.

Rabbie Burns

I thought one night I'd write a poem
I searched my head real hard
I thought the words would flow you see
And I'd be another bard.
Rabbie the second was my aim
I'll set my sights real high
But still those words refused to come
This might be pie in the sky.
I scratched my head, I chewed my pen,
I sought for inspiration
But no matter how hard, I searched for words
My brain was on vacation.
The page it stayed so clear and white
With not a scrape of a pen
Perhaps I'll have a cup of tea
And then I'll start again.
I've had my tea, a slice of toast
And a walk around the room
But still my head was empty
And I was filled with gloom.
Now after weeks and weeks of trying
I've come to this conclusion,
Another Burns, I'll never be
It was just sheer delusion.
So now instead, I'll read the poems,
That are written in the book
As I've discovered, it is too hard
It's easier just to look.

Sammy My Pet Snail

I want to tell ye all this tale,
About wee Sammy, my pet snail.
There's just one thing that he did lack,
He had nae hoose upon his back.

Noo a snail without a hoose is sad
A felt real sorry for that lad,
I tried to see what I could do,
I'm sure that you would do that too.

I saw a notice, homes for sale,
I showed it to ma wee pet snail.
He said I think I'll join the queue
For that home I have to view.

He joined the queue that very day
But I am very sad to say,
When at last his walk was done,
The houses all alas had gone.

But there's a happy ending to this tale
A said to Sammy, my pet snail,
My tortoise Beth has room to spare
And if you want, you two can share.

So now it is a house for two,
Both of them can share the view.
The happiest bit o' the tale for me,
Is Sammy now can live rent free.

Something For Free

Walking past the city hall,
I saw a great big queue,
I wonder what they're waiting for,
I'll maybe join it too.

Something for free, the notice said,
Whatever can it be.
I'll simply wait until my turn,
Then I will surely see.

The queue it moved at quite a pace,
I was nearly at the door.
Very soon it was my turn
As they shouted out two more.

There were two nurses in the room,
I got an awful fright,
When the nurse picked up the needle,
It was a fearsome sight.

Roll up your sleeve, now don't be scared,
I need a clearer view.
For the queue that I had joined outside,
Was for the annual jab for flu.

Tam And Eck And Me

Tam and Eck and me one day,
All met up tae go oot tae play,
But we couldnae decide what to do
As each of us had a point of view.

Wee Tam he wanted tae play on his bike
That wis something he really did like
But last time we did, we had a crash
It really created a big stramash.

For Eck he crashed intae a tree
Then fell off and skinned his knee,
A couldnae stop an fell on him
A really thought a had broken a limb.

A scrambled up and tried tae stand
Blood wis pourin fae ma hand
A didnae see Tam comin close
Till a felt a crack across ma nose.

Tam landed heavily on his head
I thought at first that he wis dead
But then he gave an awful yell
It's a your fault that a fell.

Ma bikes all bent an it wis brand new
A really don't know what to do
When a get hame an tell ma dad
He'll say you two are always bad.

Tam And Eck And Me

Then Eck he said a want to choose
When we make a pick, I always lose,
A want tae go an fly ma kite
Surely that will be all right.

We said last time we flew a kite
We really got an awful fright
Our kites took off intae the air
Where we ran we didnae care.

We ran really fast across the gress
Where we were we couldnae care less
But suddenly we saw some coos
This really wis no good news.

But it got worse, when we heard a roar
We tried tae run though our legs were sore
A muckle bull wis runnin fast
A thought this day could be our last.

But just as we were startin to tire
We spotted a fence made o' barbed wire,
And as that bull started tae tower
We very quickly scrambled ower.

Our claes were torn intae shreds
And the three o' us got sent tae oor beds.
A don't think we'll risk that again
It brought tae us too much pain.

Tam And Eck And Me

The choice today it would be mine
A thought tae masel that will be fine,
We'll tak a walk doon tae the wood
A think that will be really good.

So off tae the wood we swiftly ran
Ma pals they said, that's a great plan,
We reached the trees an ran in quick
Then we found the trees were really thick.

It got real dark an we couldnae see
Where we were it worried me,
Ma pals ran on deeper still
They thought tae thersel this is a thrill.

They didnae know a wis scared o' the dark
An really wisnae enjoyin this lark,
Ma heart wis beatin in ma breast
And a felt a panic in ma chest.

A wis scared we'd hae tae stay all night
When ahead I saw a welcome sight.
It was a sign with exit on
And all at once my fears were gone.

We hurried on along the track
And I knew that we would soon be back
An I wouldnae have to confess my fear
As I knew my pals would only jeer.

The Beach

The sun wis shining brightly one day
My maw said go away oot an play
I decided I would go doon tae the sea
A lot o' fun I thought it wid be.

Ma maw packed up some food tae eat
An a bottle o' water because o' the heat,
But I'm warning you little Billy
Don't you dare do anything silly.

It wis a good walk doon tae the sea,
So I set off smartly, feeling free,
I thought tae myself, I'll sing a song
That will help as I journey along.

As I sang, my mouth was open real wide
When a fly decided tae go inside,
The thought o' that fly, made me sick
So I spat it out really quick.

Nae mair singing was ma plan
I'll just try to whistle if I can.
I started off in great belief
But not a sound came through my teeth.

At last I saw the sea ahead
I'll go and paddle in the sea instead
So I put ma bag doon with great care
But of one thing I wis unaware.

The Beach

A great big dug had saw ma bag
An wi lots o' speed it didnae lag,
An it made off wi a' ma food
I knew myself that wisnae good.

It ran a bit then stopped tae bark
As if tae say a'm havin a lark,
I ran real fast tae catch that dug
Bit it just treated me like a mug.

Each time it stopped, I thought I'd won
But that clever dug it wisnae done,
An tae prove its point, gave me a fright
When it quickly ran right oot o' sight.

I had chased that dug, for quite a while
I must have run for over a mile,
I didnae know what I could do
As I didnae recognise the view.

If I can't get hame, I'll get in strife
Then I saw a man and his lady wife,
An I ran across tae ask for help
The man heard ma tale, an gave a yelp.

That dug o' ours is just a pest
My patience he just wants tae test,
He does this every other day
With people he only wants tae play.

The Beach

Just come tae our hoose an get some tea
Eat as much as ye want, all for free
An spend some time wi our silly hound
We should have left him in that pound.

Ma wife felt sorry when she saw his eyes
So we made a decision that wasnae wise,
We can take him home, he can be oor pet
But we havenae managed tae train him yet.

Paper, leather, clothes or wood
That dug treats everything as food,
The bills that a get fae the vet
Make him a very expensive pet.

Then suddenly the dug cam hame
Limpin like it wis very lame,
The man he said, do not worry
He only does it tae make us feel sorry.

When the dug saw me he ran right over
Just say tae the laddie, ye are sorry, Rover,
So it ran across an gave me a kiss
Wi a sloppy tongue that couldnae miss.

Then the man he said as its sae late
I'll tak ye hame tae yer gate,
So ma paddle in the sea a didnae reach
When I went for ma trip doon tae the beach

The Berry Picking

I went to the berries, to earn some cash,
But that decision was a wee bit rash.
I learned a lesson that week because,
You'll never guess how hard it was.

On Monday I went to pick some rasps,
Held them gently in my clasp,
But the juice it ran right down my arm.
I must be doing these berries harm.

Tuesday was the strawberry pickin,
Soon I was my fingers lickin.
More o' them went doon ma throat
Than that poor farmer's basket got.

Gooseberries were my Wednesday task,
He should have given us gloves and mask.
The thorns they tore ma skin to shreds.
This is worse than the strawberry beds.

Blackcurrants were the Thursday choice,
At first I started to rejoice.
No thorns today or beds of straw.
But they're the smallest fruit you ever saw.

Ma basket took all day to fill.
I surely dinnae hae the skill.
This berry pickin doesnae pay,
A'll need to find some other way.

The Boat Trip

I opened up the window
It's a lovely summer day,
I think I'll just get up an dressed
And get away and oot tae play.

I shouted on ma wee pal Jim
As he is a clever lad,
He'll maybe keep me oot o' trouble
And keep me safe fae dad.

My dad he is a great big lad
An he sometimes can be cruel,
Whenever he discovers
I have broken another rule.

We'll go and watch some people fish
So we set off doon tae the pier,
But the men they quickly told us
Don't you come too near.

This water is too dangerous
And its really very deep
And the drop into the water
You'll find is very steep.

So we stood right back tae watch them
But it really wis nae fun,
We'll have tae try something else
Tae enjoy with all this sun.

The Boat Trip

We spied a ramp ontae a boat
We can maybe have a look,
So on we went tae explore below
And forgot how long we took.

Then we heard the engines startin up
An we thought we'd better hide,
As maybe the folk would ask us
Why are you two inside.

So we went behind a curtain
An found it was a bed,
We were tired wi our exertions
And decided to rest our head.

But we fell asleep an time moved on
Then we wakened with a start,
As suddenly we realised
We hadnae been too smart.

We climbed oot and went tae look
For the men upon that boat
They said have you any idea
How long we've been afloat.

Yer folk will be up tae ninety nine
Wonderin where ye've gone
But luckily for the pair o' you
This boat has got a phone.

The Caterpillar

I saw a big fat caterpillar
Climbing up a stalk,
A picked it off real carefully
To take it for a walk.

A put it in ma pocket
An forgot that it wis there,
And as I got undressed for bed
A put ma troosers on the chair.

Then off a went tae bed that night
Tae have a lovely dream,
But suddenly wis awakened
By a terrifying scream.

Ma maw had gone tae wash ma clothes
An the pockets she went through
An in among the other stuff
That caterpillar she did view.

Up the stairs she quickly ran
Just wait until tomorrow
When yer father finishes wi his belt
Some cushions you will need to borrow.

The China Cat

It wis a present tae yer maw,
The ugliest thing ye ever saw
Who ever bought a thing like that,
A great, big, silly, china cat.

Its head wis big,its body wee,
Noo that's not right ye will agree,
The legs were bandy, short and fat,
On that great, big, silly, china cat.

The tail it curled round and round,
The end of it I never found,
It just lay there nice and flat,
On that great, big, silly, china cat.

A problem with the eyes I saw,
An it also had a funny jaw,
It sure wis nae aristocrat,
That great, big, silly, china cat.

It had a grin, from side to side,
On a gapin mouth, held open wide,
A wondered what it wis laughin at,
That great, big, silly, china cat.

Tommy Cooper I will be,
Do some tricks, just like he.
So I dropped the cat, just like that.
And that wis the end of the china cat.

The China Teapot

One day when I was just a lad
I stuck my finger in the teapot spout
And no matter how hard I tried
I could not pull it out.

I shouted out come help me maw,
Ma fingers getting sair.
She tugged and tugged, but tugged in vain
Until I couldnae stand nae mair.

She got some butter from the dish
And melted it real fast
She tried to pour it in the spout
But ma finger wouldnae let it past.

She tugged and tugged a wee bit mair
But still with no success.
I'll shout yer faither fae oot the back,
He'll no be pleased I guess.

He had some work he had to do,
He wanted nae disruption,
Now thanks to you and that silly pot
He'll hae an interruption.

I just know he'll be right mad,
And start to yell and shout
And all because you stupid lad
Stuck your finger in that spout.

The China Teapot

Ma faither cam in wi a can o oil,
And tried a squirt or two,
We'll just leave that for a wee bit while
To see what that can do.

But the oil dripped out on ma maws good cloth,
You should have heard her yell.
Ye muckle stummer, look what you've done,
Ye're a great big gowk as well.

Nae wonder Billy's a stupid fool,
Have'n a faither thick as you,
When a think o' the stupid things ye've done,
There's not a brain between you two.

It's just as well that I have sense,
For we need a resolution,
We'll tak him roond tae the fire brigade,
Maybe they will have a solution.

The fireman looked at the china pot,
And tapped it wi a spanner.
Ma maw yelled oot, that's ma best pot,
It cost me twelve and a tanner.

But wi the tap o' the spanner it broke in bits,
And landed on the flair.
I just jumped and said in glee,
Ma fingers no stuck any mair

The Day It Was So Cauld And Snell

The day it was so cauld and snell
It made me feel no very well.
Ma nose was turnin very blue
And from it dreeps were falling too.

I stamped my feet to keep them warm
You'ld think that that would do no harm,
But then the sole fell aff ma shoe,
What on earth am I gonnae do.

I got myself a bit o' string,
That will be the very thing,
Roond ma shoe I tied it well,
Nobody will ever tell.

But I forgot to cut the string,
Wasn't that a stupid thing,
For ma other foot stood on the lace
And before I knew I was on my face.

My face it now felt red with heat,
As I lay there in the street
And as I slowly reached my feet
A crowd all cheered, repeat, repeat.

Now wasn't that a sorry tale
It's sad enough to make ye wail,
Sure enough I hear you cry,
It'll bring a tear to a glassy eye.

The Dunce's Cap

When I was asked to write for you,
I chose this little page of white.
The words they were so hard to write
As I tried to think of something bright.

I had no inspiration,
I scanned right through my mind.
My brain you see had gone on strike
And nothing I could I find.

I sat down in my easy chair
I'll try another way,
But once again I found alas
There were no words to say.

I read right through my paper,
I studied every letter,
But once again to my dismay,
I found this was no better.

I took to bed, I hid my head
I felt like such a fool.
Then all at once, I knew just why,
I wore the dunce's cap at school.

The Fitba

I wanted tae learn some fitba
So I joined the local teams
But I very soon discovered
It's no as easy as it seems.

I started runnin doon the field
Prancing like a foal
I knew that I wis playin well
When I kicked it in the goal.

Ya muckle clown, what have ye done
Ma team cried wi' a roar
Dae ye no have any sense
It's at the other end, ye have to score.

I tried again, I ran real fast
But I wisnae quite aware
Of this great big hulkin superman
He gave me quite a scare.

He gave a shove, an doon a went
And landed on ma face.
But a didnae know a dug had been
And done its business in that place.

A quickly got up tae ma feet
Ma legs were getting sair
Ma back wis achin, a wis oot o' breath
A don't want tae play this any mair.

The Fitba

But a picked up the ball and took a run
Then swiftly let it fly
The ball went sailing up the park
And hit the ref right in the eye.

He quickly raced across the pitch
He wisnae well amused at me
Ye think its funny dae ye son
You'll no be getting off scot free

So he marchit me right off that pitch
A've got the very job for you
So he dressed me in the mascot suit
Now a look like a gorilla in the zoo.

The Funfair

The funfair came tae visit oor toon
I said tae ma dad, please tak us doon.
He said in a voice, that wis real grave
Only if ye promise tae behave.

So off we went doon tae the fair,
Runnin fast without a care.
Just watch out, ye don't get lost
Or you'll find yersel countin the cost.

We first went on a wee green train
An asked our dad can we do that again.
Then we saw some horses, prancing high
We said tae dad, can we gie that a try.

Then off tae a stall, that used a gun
That looks tae be a lot o fun,
A paid ma money and took ma aim
A dinnae think a understood the game.

A didnae know some things were a prize
And tae the stallholders great surprise
Ma aim wis very good that night
And I fired at that shelf fae left tae right.

The prizes broke in a thousand bits
A wis really pleased wi a ma hits,
But it cost ma dad thirty quid
For all the damage that a did.

The Heidie

When a wis a lad an very young
A liked tae play the fool
I thought that I would maybe try
A trick one day at school.

I tied a string tae the heidie's door
I thought it would be fun
As I knew the way I tied it
There wis nowhere he could run.

A went aboot ma daily tasks
And forgot what a had done
Very soon it wis four o'clock
And ma day at school wis gone.

A had ma tea, then a went oot
Tae join ma pals at play
All too soon ma maw cried oot
Its time for bed today.

What I had forgotten
Was the heidie in his room
And had no way of knowing
Just what would be ma doom.

The heidie banged the door real hard
Can someone let me out
But there wis nobody near that room
And no-one heard him shout.

The Heidie

He spent the night upon the flair
It wis hard and very cold
When I find out, who did this
His parents will be told.

Early the next morning
The jannie spied the string.
I wonder what has happened here
This is the strangest thing.

Quickly he untied the string
And set the heidie free
I have to find the blighter
Who did this to me.

He looked around and saw some gum
Lying on the ground,
He gave a scowl and quickly said
The culprit I have found.

There's only one lad, in this school
Who dares to eat gum here
I'll quickly go round to his house
And fill him full of fear.

When the knock cam tae the door
The heidie marched right in
An' said tae ma dad, this little lad
Has committed quite a sin.

The Heidie

There's one thing I can tell you
A lesson I learned that day
For every stupid thing you do
There is a price to pay

The Folly Of drink

It was a dark and dreary night,
When suddenly I got a fright.
I looked in a mirror on the wa'
You'll never guess just what I saw.

A face it looked right back at me,
I asked myself, who can it be.
I think I've seen that face before.
I thought as I ran oot the door

A glanced over my shoulder as I ran
Just try to catch me if you can.
My knees were like a knocker chappin,
The sweat wis aff me fairly drappin.

Now right ahead and in ma door,
Then I drappit on the floor.
That whisky sure can tell a tale,
Tomorrow night, I'll stick to ale.

The Jumble Sale

I went tae a jumble sale today
To see what I could buy,
I wandered round the tiny stalls
To see if something caught my eye.

Then suddenly I was aware
Of a teddy on a shelf
It looked so sad and lonely
As it sat there by itself.

One ear was hanging by a thread
And its coat was really bare,
But I fell in love with that teddy
And was completely unaware.

It had some stuffing hanging out
And it only had one eye,
But I loved that little teddy
And that bear I had to buy.

I took it home real careful
And showed it to my maw,
I'll just get out my sewing box
And quickly mend his paw.

She said I'll sew back on his ear
And give him two new eyes
Tomorrow when you waken up
You'll get a nice surprise.

The Jumble Sale

The next day when I wakened up
Lying there upon my bed,
Was my teddy in a jumper
And a hat upon his head.

My maw had made some clothes for him
And I knew they'd keep him warm
I told him that I loved him
And would keep him safe from harm.

My bear still sits upon a shelf
But he does not sit alone
My toys all sit around him
And his lonely days are gone.

The Lentil Soup

I thought I'd make the tea one night
An' give ma maw a treat
She had gone oot for an hour or two
Tae visit a woman doon the street.

A pot o' soup that would be fine,
I'll put some lentils in the pot,
I wisnae sure how much tae use
So I just put in the lot.

I chopped the veggies nice an fine
An added them tae the watter
I turned the gas up tae full
I thought it widnae matter.

A decided a would go oot the back
An play there for a while.
A knew that from experience
That soup took a time tae bile.

But when a went back in, a got a shock,
That soup had a' biled ower,
I knew when maw, saw the mess
That she would really glower.

Then I noticed an awful smell
My stomach nearly turned.
I knew that trouble I really was in
As her pot was badly burned.

The Lentil Soup

I turned off the gas and took the pot
And emptied it in the sink.
But once again being me
A didnae take the time tae think.

That pot o soup, wis awful thick
An it chokit up the drain
An a knew ma maw would be real mad
If she needed the plumber roond again

A knew that last time he cam roond
He just undid some screws,
So a thought that if a tried
A could save her a bob or two.

So I went beneath the sink
And the screws I did undo
But I forgot I needed a basin
And ower the floor the mess all flew.

Then I heard some words fae ma maw
An I knew that I wis caught
If I could send kids back tae a shop
Then another one I would have bought

The Midgies

There wis a cloud o' midgies
Buzzin round ma head
And the very sight o' them
Filled me full of dread.

I knew what thought wis in their heads
As down they looked at me,
I would be an ideal snack
That they could have for tea.

All at once they gave a swoop
And they came hurtling down
All over me they settled
From ma feet up to my crown.

I tried and tried so very hard
To fend off their attack,
But more and more I felt them bite
I must have been the perfect snack.

My arms were lashing right and left
As I tried to fend them off,
But the harder that I hit them
More of my blood they'd scoff.

I grabbed a fern from the ground
And waved it fast around
But it didnae make a difference
I very quickly found.

The Midgies

I now was very itchy
And really had to scratch
So I started to outrun them
But fell in a nettle patch.

I went lookin for some dockens
But tripped ower a little mound,
When lots o' beasties ran fae it
I knew an ant hill I had found.

I said tae myself a've had enough
I'll just go hame for ma tea
But as a walked up tae ma door
A wis stung wi a bumble bee.

So that's the end o' ma sorry tale
They say things come in three.
But I am sorry, I have tae say
Its only in bad things, they come tae me

The Plum Tree

Ma next door neighbour had a tree,
Wi the bonniest plums you'll ever see.
One day as I walked doon the street,
One o' them landed at ma feet.

I picked it up and took a bite,
It quickly disappeared from sight.
That plum it wis so rare and sweet,
I'd like another wan to eat.

I stood on his wall and raised ma arm,
I didnae think I wis doin harm,
There were dozens o' plums upon that tree,
He could surely spare me two or three

But ma neighbour suddenly opened his door,
Then let oot an almighty roar.
Ye thieving tyke, I know yer name,
I'll just tak ye tae yer hame.

I took aff like a thing possessed,
That I wis feart ye've maybe guessed.
Ma feet fair rattled doon the street,
I hope nae polis I will meet.

But ma neighbour he ran fast an a',
I hoped that he wid maybe fa',
For every minute, he wis makin ground
An getting nearer when I looked around.

The Plum Tree

Then all at once I got a fright,
As I felt ma collar pullin tight.
Ma neighbour had it in his hand,
It felt just like a metal band.

His face it wis a sight tae see,
As he stood scowling down on me.
Each eye stood out, like on a stalk,
He wis sae mad, he couldnae talk.

He quickly hauled me aff ma feet
And then he dragged me up the street.
I knew that I'd soon reach ma fate,
When just ahead I saw ma gate.

A winnae tell ye what wis said,
Before once more a wis sent tae bed.
But if ye ever steal forbidden fruit,
Make sure it's not from that nasty brute.

The Rag Man

Things to sell, things to sell.
One day I heard the rag man yell.
There were lots of treats for a lad to see
But he wouldnae gi me owt for free.

Glassy bools of brilliant shades,
Little knives with folding blades.
Floating balloons tied to his cart,
Ye widnae know just where to start.

When I said to the man, a had nae cash.
He said don't get yersel in such a fash,
Just bring some rags and you will see,
That you can get something for free.

I went in ma door and up ma stairs.
I'll take ma socks, I've lots o pairs,
I'll stick them in a bag or two,
I really hope that they will do.

I took them out to the rag man's cart.
For a wee bit lad, yer awful smart.
He handed me a red balloon
Hope to see ye again right soon.

I soon found out, that I wisnae wise.
They 're the only socks in the hoose ma size,
And now when I play in the street.
I'm the only laddie wi bare feet.

The Sniffly Nose

A had a cold an a sniffly nose
A must have caught the flu
A didnae have a hankie
An a didnae know what a could do.

So I wiped ma sleeve below ma nose
Then a had tae use it mair.
A knew when a got hame that day,
Ma maw wid be aware.

And right enough when a went in
She asked whats that upon yer sleeve,
When I replied I did not know
She said your words I don't believe.

I brought ye up tae tell the truth
And not tell a pack of lies,
I thought you had learned by this time
There's nothing wrong with ma eyes.

If there's nothing there upon that sleeve
You can wear it tomorrow to school
And all the kids will laugh at you
And call you a silly fool.

So I told her the truth
About what I had done
And she said to me, don't ever lie
Then I can proudly call you son.

The Swaying Room

Ma heid wis poundin, I'd swallied a few
The whisky had gone down a treat.
But now ma stomach wis swirlin round
And I needed a new pair o feet.

They wouldnae go in unison.
I staggered left and right.
I couldnae work out what wis wrong.
I got an awful fright.

But then I lookit across the room
And it wis very strange.
For there wis two of everything
I thought I was deranged.

I tried to speak, but woe is me
My tongue was stuck right fast.
I struggled very manfully
And I got it free at last.

No-one could make out what I said
My brain and mouth were out of sync
So ma friends all said, go hame tae bed
You've had too much tae drink.

The Sweetie Shop

A ran doon, tae the sweetie shop
A had a penny a could spend.
The sweeties were enticing
As I looked fae end tae end.

Lucky tatties, aniseed balls
White mice wi wee pink eyes,
Dolly mixtures, toffee bars
Even bags that said surprise.

A thought tae masel, what will a choose
As a looked about some more,
Auld Geordie said, mak up yer mind
Afore a throw ye oot the door.

A'll hae tae go oot tae the back
A've something a must do.
So aff he went without a glance
And disappeared from view.

Then suddenly a saw a pile
Of sticky, toffee, chewy sweets
If I am quick, a can eat some up
And then auld Geordie a can cheat.

And at that very clever thought
Ma mooth began tae watter
That it really wis dishonest
Tae me just didnae matter.

The Sweetie Shop

So a grabbed masel, a couple o' sweets
And shoved them in ma mooth
Suddenly Geordie came back through
And said now tell tae me the truth.

What have ye done while a wis gone
I want ye now to open yer jaw
If you hae stolen any o' ma sweets
I'll tak ye hame an tell yer maw.

A tried real hard to open ma mooth
But ma teeth were stuck real fast
A tried real hard, but all in vain
Ma die wis really cast.

He locked his shop an took me hame
An banged at ma hoose door.
This theivin tyke has stole ma sweets
He won't be welcome any more.

Then off he went and left me there
Tae the mercy o' ma maw
She took one great almighty swipe
And skelped me round the jaw

But the saddest bit about this tale
Wis the toffee broke a tooth
An very soon a wis in a chair
As the dentist lookit in ma mooth.

The Sweetie Shop

He looked at ma teeth and grinning said
There a lot of work tae do
By the time that I have done wi you
You'll be wishin you had left that chew.

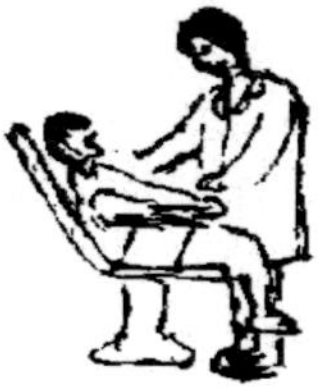

The Icy Blast

I sheltered from the icy blast
The wind blew fierce and cold
I drew my coat in closer
I must be getting old.

I need a coat two sizes big
To cover all my clothes
A pack of tissues in my hand
To use to wipe my nose.

I think I'd better stay inside
Until its better weather
And maybe sit and get a verse
From yours truly, its my faither

The Swimming Pool

I stood at the side of the swimming pool,
Just looking at the watter,
I couldnae swim at all ye see,
But I thought that widnae matter.

I'll take ma time, I winnae rush,
No one will take me for a fool,
But as I stood in trepidation,
A laddie shoved me in the pool.

He shoved so hard, I flew right in,
I landed with a splatter
And like a stone, I dropped and fell.
To the bottom o' that watter.

A opened up ma mooth tae shout,
That wis a big mistake.
A swallowed nearly half the pool,
I thought for goodness sake.

Did no-one see me as I fell,
Please can someone get me out,
But I'll just have to wait and see,
For I cannot use my voice to shout.

Ma eyes and ears began to pop,
I felt like such a fool,
But suddenly I heard a noise,
As a man jumped in the pool.

The Swimming Pool

He quickly dragged me to the top,
My limbs were flappin round,
But suddenly I drew a breath
And guess what I had found.

I did not sink, I floated on,
I was feeling very dim,
But from that day I always found,
That I knew how to swim.

The Sore Toe

Ma toe wis sore one day
A couldnae go oot tae play,
A wis runnin aboot without ma shoes
Ran intae a table an got a bruise.

It wis a horrible shade o' black an blue
An a coulnae even get on ma shoe.
An a wis scared a would hurt it again
As a didnae want tae get mair pain.

A thought a wis safe in the hoose
But ma wee brother wis on the loose.
An he stepped doon hard on ma toe
An a fairly told him where to go.

The Tadpoles

I went one day doon tae the pond
It wisnae really far
I took ma net an got some spawn
And put it in a jar.

I took it home real careful
And put it in a sink,
If I just watch over it
I'll get some tadpoles I think.

I went out and looked each day
Until one day I saw,
Lots of little tadpoles
An I ran tae show ma maw.

They'll grow intae great dirty frogs
That ye know a couldnae stand
You'll have tae go an tak them back
An' remove them from this land.

But I knew I couldnae tak them back
They were like friends tae me,
I'll need tae find another place
Where they can safely be.

So I looked and found another spot
I know they'll be safe here.
But I cannae tell my mother
As she made things very clear.

The Tadpoles

Then I heard a scream fae in the hoose
And my maw she gave a shout
Look what happened when I used the tap
These tadpoles all shot out.

I had only used the water tank
That fed intae the hoose
Ye stupid little scunner
Its no safe tae let ya loose.

The Ode Tae Leila

Ah cam the night to talk to you two,
And found it far from boring,
But all ma thoughts were drowned right out,
By that wee Leila's snoring.

She is a model cat for sure,
Just right in every degree.
But that's the thought in Lisbeths head
And its not shared by me.

For killin mice she might be fine
She maybe has her uses.
But dinnae try to talk me round
Am no listenin to yer excuses.

The Tartan Breeks

Ma maw bought me some tartan breeks
In shades of yellow, blue and green
I looked at them in horror
The brightest breeks ye have ever seen.

Next day she made me wear them
When I went oot tae play
I hid from all my pals from school
As I knew what they would say.

So I went intae the wash hoose
And I stuck them in the sink
I used some boiling water
As I hoped the breeks would shrink.

But the breeks were made o' real good cloth
And they came oot good as new,
I'll have to put on my thinking cap
To try to work out what else I can do.

I put them on and started out
Dripping water as I went
Suddenly I saw some men
Mixing piles o' wet cement.

The very answer was the thought
That came into ma head,
But the men they knew what I planned to do
And chased me away instead.

The Tartan Breeks

We cannae let you spoil these breeks
For everybody needs a laugh
Tae share in a the fun they'll get
We've intervened on their behalf.

Yer maw must sure be colour blind
Tae send ye oot in those
Or they must have been a bargain lot
If those are what she chose.

A ran off fast tae hide ma shame
And a thought cam tae ma head
A'll nip back hame an get the key
There's a pot o paint in ma dads shed.

The paint wis a lovely shade o black
And a coat or two will do
Now ma breaks are painted black
Not yellow, green and blue.

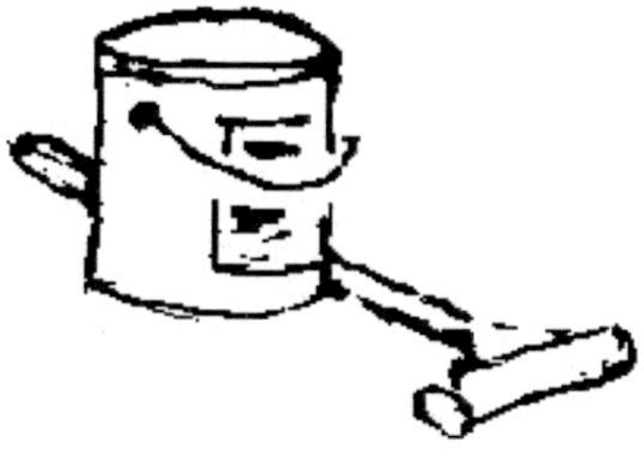

The Tattie Pickin

When a wis young an needin some cash
At the tattie pickin a'll gie it a bash,
A thought tae masel, how hard can it be
A'll visit the farm, an then a can see.

Ye can start this Monday, my young man
You'll get collected by my van,
It'll pick ye up at half past eight
Just mak sure ye are nae late.

Monday came an a got the van
Doon tae the farm it quickly ran,
We a' got oot an started tae walk
There certainly wis nae time tae talk.

There stood a digger, shiny and green
And the biggest field ye've ever seen.
There had tae be a hundred row
And in each one, potatoes grow.

A chose a row and we started out
The man in charge, he gave a shout,
Get a basket and pick those spuds
Just make sure ye pick nae duds.

That digger it went doon real fast
A wisnae sure how long a wid last.
A bent ma back an started tae pick
A didnae think it wid be this quick.

The Tattie Pickin

But a bent ma back an ma fingers flew
Its nice tae learn something new.
But ma back wisnae used tae a' the bendin
An the pain it gave wisnae pretendin.

The ground wis heavy and very wet
A never knew the pain ye could get,
Rakin through that dirty soil
Just tae get some potatoes tae boil.

Ma back had now gone into shock
An I realized it had started tae lock.
Ma feet were cold an ma hands were sore
I don't think a can do this any more.

Then the man called out, time for a break
A cup of tea ye all can take.
Get oot yer piece an eat it fast
Ye'll find yer break, will nae last.

Soon it wis time tae start again
A don't think a'll ever forget the pain
As a heard more shouts fae that man
I thought tomorrow I won't be on that van.

The time arrived when a got hame
Ma back will never be the same
Then ma maw she happily said tae me
A've got some lovely potatoes for yer tea

The Turning Tide

One day I went down to the beach,
The water was well out of reach.
A distance away, I saw some land.
I think I can reach it across the sand.

So I started to walk out to the sea,
What an adventure, this will be.
Just wait until I tell ma maw,
Of all the wonders that I saw.

I carried on without a care,
Of any danger, was unaware,
That land it wisnae getting nearer.
A didnae see its shape nae clearer.

But suddenly then I became aware,
That the sand it wisnae there nae mair.
The water lappit round ma legs,
It gave to me an awful fleg.

A turned around and tried to run,
Ma ordeal it had just begun,
For all around there just was sea.
That water it had trickit me.

A rock I saw just to my right,
It really was a welcome sight.
I scrambled on and skinned ma knee,
This wisnae how it was meant to be.

The Turning Tide

I sat for hours upon that rock.
Watchin the time, on a distant clock.
I wonder how long I'll have to stay.
I hope that I get hame the day.

My stomach ached through lack of food
A really wisnae feelin good.
I wish this morning ma breakfast I ate
If I had it now, I'd clean ma plate.

I saw a man, walkin on the sand.
I stood up tall and waved ma hand.
I hope he'll see and know a'm stuck.
That really would be a piece of luck.

Stay there he shouted in a very loud voice.
As if a wis there through freedom of choice.
I'll just get a boat and row out to you,
I'll be over there in a minute or two.

He pulled the oars, wi the greatest of ease.
When I saw that boat, I wis real pleased.
Now very soon I'll be back on dry land.
An glad when ma feet are back on the sand.

This dangerous tale, I kept to myself.
I knew it wouldnae go doon well.
I just told ma maw I had got lost.
I knew what the truth would be tae ma cost.

Walking The Dug

One day when I cam hame fae school
A wis messing aboot, an playing the fool
Maw said, gie me a rest fae that stupid talk
And tak the dug oot for a walk.

But don't be late she said to me
Mind be back in time for tea,
For if yer late at comin in
Ye'll find yer tea is in the bin.

So a got ma coat and grabbed the lead
That should be all that I will need
Oot the door and doon the street
A wonder who today a'll meet.

A set off at quite a pace
A thought the dug a could maybe race
A undid its lead and set it free
A just hope that it comes back to me.

But off it ran, like a shot fae a gun
It thought tae itsel, a'll have some fun
So it ran inside a wifie's gate
A thought tae masel, this isnae great.

She wis peggin her washin on the line
Things were really goin fine,
But ma dug he thought, lets have some fun
A'm sure she winnae miss just one.

Walking The Dug

So he ran at the basket and took his choice
Then the wifie suddenly found her voice
She yelled at him, just put that doon
That's only ma best Sunday goon.

But ma dug wis oot for fun that day
And he really only wanted tae play
So he just ran through between her legs
An made her drop her basket o pegs.

The goon wis flappin like a sheet
As he ran roond and roond her feet
He tripped her up an doon she fell
Letting oot an awful yell.

Ma dug got a fright, an off he went
On more adventure, he wis bent
The goon wis sailin in the air
But ma wee dug, he didnae care.

He pelted off into the wood
By now a wisnae feelin good
I've had enough, now just behave
Or a'll end up in an early grave.

But he still ran and with his eye
A rabbit hole he did espy,
And doon he went at quite a pace
How can I get him out o that place.

Walking The Dug

A shouted him till a wis hoarse
But he wis havin fun of course
Please just come out, I said in fear
But he just pretended he couldnae hear.

If a go hame an tell ma maw
She'll no be very pleased at a',
Shell send ye tae a home for dugs
And gie me a skelp roond both ma lugs.

Then a man come strollin roond the bend
A thought maybe he, some help would lend
So a said to him, ma dugs doon there
But he said tae me, do you think a care.

He then walkit off really fast
Ma mooth fell open, quite aghast
Ya muckle lout, ma dug is scared
But he walked off as he never cared.

What can I do, so I just sat doon
And spied a corner o' the goon.
A tuggit hard and gave a heave
But I only rippit aff a sleeve.

So I tried again an gave a tug
Oot came the goonie and the dug
A got oot its lead really fast
And got it safely tied at last.

Walking The Dug

A thought a dug would be nae bother
That we could look out for each other
But that wifie will go tae ma mother's door
And let ma mother know the score.

A'll be sent tae bed without ma tea,
You'll be nae better off than me
She'll tak ye oot intae the shed
Then that will always be yer bed.

Pit A Pat, Pit A Pat

Pit a pat, pit a pat,
I saw a stupid pussy cat
It tried to go through a skinny gate
An it got stuck, cos it was too fat.

I gave it a kick wi my number tens
An it shot oot quick and fast,
It turned around and gave a yell
Thank goodness I am free at last.

But just you watch, you nasty man
One day I'll get you back,
For when you least expect it
That's when I will attack.

Washing Day

My maw wis way doon tae the shops,
I knew she'd be a while,
I thought that I would help her oot,
Put the washin on tae bile.

I sorted a' the colours oot,
One bundle a' wis white
I'd seen her dae that lots o' times,
I knew that I wis right.

The whites I put into the tub,
Some powder I did add,
I shut the lid, leave it to boil,
I was a clever lad.

Then I thought it was the time
To rinse them in the sink,
But when I looked into the tub,
The whites had a' gone pink.

In ma rush a' missed a sock
A lovely shade of red.
Ma faithers vests were baby pink,
An the sheets fae aff the bed.

Then my maw cam in the door,
I won't say what she said
But it wisnae only just that sock,
That was a lovely shade of red.

What's For Tea

A wis invited for a meal one day
By the wife that lived next door.
But as she dished up on the plate
Some fell upon the floor.

She picked it up an gave it a wipe
My floor is really clean
She placed it down upon my plate
And I suddenly a wisnae keen.

She said eat up, now don't be shy
As she put ma cutlery doon,
But I suddenly lost ma appetite
As a saw her lick ma spoon.

A looked real close upon that plate
And in the cabbage, I did see
Staring up with beady eyes
A caterpillar gazing at me.

I'll have tae think o' some excuse
I really couldnae stay,
So I pretended I wis feelin sick
And would return another day.

Noo ma maw isnae the best o' cooks
And her cookin is quite plain
But after ma visit tae next door
I'll never complain of her food again.

When I Was A Laddie At The School

When I wis a laddie at the school,
I always seemed to play the fool.
When the teachers tested all the class.
I was the one who wouldn't pass.

I could not count from one to ten,
I'd get to five and start again
And when I tried to read and write,
My printing was an awful sight.

My spelling also fared no better,
I used to mix up every letter.
Playing sports, I'd surely fly,
But I got worse at every try.

But now at last I've found my forte,
I'm a dab hand at the shortie,
My sponges are so full of air,
Everybody wants a share.

My biscuits crunch with every bite,
My pastry is all crisp and light,
I now can count and read and write,
As I need to get my recipes right.

When I Wis Just A Wee Bit Lad

When I wis just a wee bit lad
I wandered oot ma gate,
The sun wis shining brightly
An I knew it wisnae late.

A tiny dug, ran across tae me
And tugged me by the hand,
It wanted me as a pal ye see
So ye have tae understand.

I never gave a thought tae the fact
That ma maw would maybe worry
Or of the events that would happen that day
An that I would really be sorry.

We quickly scampered up the street
As I followed that wee dug,
It tried tae hide once or twice
But I showed I wis nae mug.

I just waited till he cam back oot
Fur I knew dugs had nae brain
I knew that he would get fed up
And come back fur me again.

We carried on for quite a while
As that dug ran more and more,
But what that silly dug forgot
I had two legs but he had four.

When I Wis Just A Wee Bit Lad

Ma legs were getting very sore
An I was filled with fears,
I hope that dug knows where we are
As my eyes they filled with tears.

But the dug lay doon, as it wis tired
And quickly closed its eyes.
No matter how loud I shouted it,
It just ignored my cries.

So I just lay down beside the dug,
An I fell asleep as well,
I didn't know how long we slept
As the time a couldnae tell.

When ma maw had found the open gate
And realised that I had gone,
She had to raise the alarm
As she knew what I had done.

She called oot a' the neighbours
And phoned the polis too.
The polis came and said tae her
This is nothing new.

Ye need tae put a chain on him
Or buy a stronger gate,
But we'd better go an look for him
As we know it's getting late.

When I Wis Just A Wee Bit Lad

So a' the polis were oot in force
They were nae well amused,
Better care ye should tak o' him
Wis what she wis accused.

We've brought him back sae many times
He feels like an o' us,
A only hope fur all oor sakes
He didnae tak the bus.

So off they went in groups o' three
Searching far and wide
He only is a wee bit lad
Look fur places he can hide.

As it got dark I wakened up
An got an awful fright
If someone doesnae find me
I might be here all night.

At that thought, I started to cry
And shouted out for help,
As the polis heard, they ran to me
What you really need is a skelp.

We've wasted loads o' time on you,
You really are a pain
When yer maw gave birth tae you
You surely never got a brain.

Why Do Cats Have Claws

A question came into my mind
Perhaps the answer you may find.
Why when cats were given paws
Did they also add on claws.

My sofa it looked awful smart,
My cat thought, I know where to start.
It jumped up upon the seat
And started clawing with his feet.

The curtains were his target next,
When I looked at them, I was fair vexed
Threads were hanging, quite a few
What had it done, they were nearly new.

I also had a leather stool,
Now that wee cat it was no fool,
It lay out on that stool and stretched
And left its claw marks deeply etched.

You'll never guess what next he eyed
He gave no clue what he had spied.
I was quietly sleeping on my chair
When he came flying through the air.

It landed on me claws widespread
I was lucky that it missed my head,
But my body it looks like a maze
Covered in scratches, all over the place.

We're Drunk

Ma heid wis poundin, I'd swallied a few
The whisky had gone down a treat.
But now ma stomach wis swirlin round
And I needed a new pair o feet.

They wouldnae go in unison.
I staggered left and right.
I couldnae work out what wis wrong.
I got an awful fright.

Then I lookit across the room
And it wis very strange.
For there was two of everything
I thought I was deranged.

I tried to speak, but woe is me
My tongue was stuck right fast.
I struggled very manfully
And I got it free at last.

No-one could make out what I said
My brain and mouth were out of sync
So ma friends all said, go hame tae bed
You've had too much tae drink.

We're Finished

A've come tae the end of this little book
An I'm glad that you have had a look,
An I hope ye all have had some fun
Reading of the things I've done.

I always had a love of verse
Another way you can converse,
You just have to use your imagination
Then you will have another creation.

Your words may also start to flow
And your own collection you can grow,
So why not lift a pen today
And you may find the words to say.

I've had lots of fun filling this book
Enjoying all of the time it took.
But everything comes to an end
And to the publishers I must send.

As I wish to share my words with you
And I hope you will enjoy them too,
I know that I have had a laugh
Receiving the words on your behalf.

So for now I must lay down my pen
Till I hear from my dad once again.
So thank you dad for all the fun
And I hope your verses are not done.

ND - #0192 - 060826 - C0 - 210/148/8 - PB - 9781780353807 - Gloss Lamination